Table

M000032524

July 2006   All Rights Reserved

This
book
would never
have been possible
without the help of
Len and Michelle Leader.

If you meet them,
thank them.

If
you want
to be happily married,
you need to read between
the lines.

If you read between the
lines of this book
you will
see my wife's
handwriting.
To her everything
I do
is due.

The scribble on the sides,
that's my children.

How To Use This book

As you read through the pages of BLISS, I hope you will find many concepts with which you disagree.

If you agree with everything herein, then you have wasted your money. The paradox is, we know we need to learn a new or different way of doing things, yet simultaneously we reject anything that disagrees with us. I am sure you can see that this state of affairs is not going to get us anywhere.

If we are to learn we must be open to that which we at first reject.

After all, if we are lacking in knowledge or understanding, it is because at present we "see" that knowledge as wrong somehow. This is natural. We aren't computers. We all have a bias. But, the typical thing to do, when we meet an idea that we strongly disagree, is to reject it out of hand.

We all look out at the world and cannot understand why people can't see the truth the way we do, after all, it does seem rather obvious. One day, I had an epiphany, I realized that an awful lot of people view me as the closed minded one. Well, I thought to myself, what are the chances that I am the one who has the truth, just by chance, and everyone else is making the mistake. Hmmmm, not good odds.

So, therefore I am going to ask you to try a new technique that has helped me immensely.

When you encounter such an idea with which you disagree, mark on the side of the page, "NO." And, when you see idea you strongly agree with, mark with a "YES."

Then, after you have finished the book, go back and compare the places you marked YES with the ones you marked NO. You should find that each point of contention is answered with that which you strongly agreed. At the very least, you will see that there is a strong contradiction between the YES points and the NO points.

For more enjoyment and to make the experience a lot more meaningful, have your spouse do the same in a separate book, and even try this exercise with a group of friends, then compare all your YES points to the NO ones.

You will have a lot of fun, or better still, you will be on your way to finding BLISS in your relationships.

Why This Book Is Different

In my travels through the marriage and parenting counseling world, I noticed that for some marriage was their pet project. For others it was parenting. And of course there were those who took up golf.

There was hardly a book or a seminar or even a counselor that I could disagree with, yet I found that neither discipline helped the other. In other words, despite the fact that a person may have been the most dedicated mother or father, it didn't seem to help them become better or happier spouses. And of course visa versa. There were people who would worship their wives or husbands, yet they were getting nowhere with their children.

It seemed like they were the proverbial man in the middle of the boat, on either side were two very self destructive individuals. Each with a drill that were determined to put a hole in the bottom of the boat. These two people represent a person's role as a parent and as a spouse. If they went over to the spouse side and worked on that relationship, then it was the parental role that suffered and the boat sank. Alternatively, if they focused their energies on their children, then their marriage seemed to go down hill.

Either way they were sunk.

And so was I. Whatever I recommended to people didn't seem to help them in their overall lives. I was frustrated with the current theories on marriage and parenting that were simply not getting the results I wanted for people. So I started delving into the ancient Jewish wisdom to see if I could find a better way.

What I uncovered were remarkably simple ideas and approaches that not only got great results but were also applicable to both situations.

Soon, I wasn't teaching marriage separate from parenting but combining the two and finding that even in the most entrenched cases, almost immediate results ensued.

Not only that, but what I have found, and what hopefully you will find is that you really cannot divide the roles at all. In other words, a good parent is a good spouse.

But more than that, the real beauty of "Bliss" is that it really doesn't teach you anything new. You don't have to practice any new habits or techniques to become a great parent or spouse.

In other words this book is totally safe. It's not going to involve any new regimen or program and turn you into something you are not.

What "Bliss" does is it takes the skills you are great at, and shows you how to apply those same techniques to the other arena. If you find parenting your forte, then you use those skills for marriage, and visa versa.

"It's remarkable," say many people who attend my seminars. "I didn't know I could be such a good husband/wife - mother/father -- I really know what to do, in fact I've been doing it for years."

What Bliss shows you is that the skills you have acquired that makes you a great parent can and should be adapted to work with a spouse. Or, that which makes you a great spouse can be used to be a great parent -- you just need to be shown how.

INTRODUCTION:

The Cure For The Marriage BLUES

No one ever said *"I am not getting anything out of this relationship anymore!"*

That is, no parent ever said it.

Why is it that we "need" a return on our investment from a spouse, yet are quite happy just giving and giving and giving to a child?

Picture this scene:

A teenage boy comes home very late from an evening out with his friends to find his mother waiting, nervously.

She calls him over for one of those annoying little talks about responsibility and how growing up in the 60's taught her to care for each other, and other such concepts that the average teenager cannot comprehend.

At some point the mother in total frustration exclaims, "Listen son, I am just not getting anything out of this relationship."

The son jolts, as though waking from a nap, and says, "you know Mom, **neither am I.**" "How about a little more allowance and I would really like it if you could fix me dinner now, I am starved."

I hope you get the point.

This isn't funny, because it would never happen. No mother this side of Neptune would ever think that her son has a brain cell that has her name on it and that he should consider her wellbeing.

Now before you get bent out of shape defending your children, please be aware of two points. One, this is a bit of an exaggeration, and it's also normal for today's children in the western world. Unless your children are shown a model of extreme giving then it's hard for a child to consider sacrificing for a parent.

Look at it from the child's point of view. You do nothing to get free air. If one day the government started taxing you to breathe, would you be outraged?

I think yes.

Well, that's kind of how children see it. They are taken care of for many years, their every whim is catered to, now you are asking for something back.

A student of mine once asked me, "I don't understand my son (the son was about 10 at the time), he just doesn't seem to comprehend that in this world you have to be responsible. No one owes you a living; you have to work hard to enjoy the good things in life."

"Well" I said. "Let me ask you, did your son ever come home and find the door locked and you told him he had to sleep in the back yard and eat grass tonight?"

This father was shocked that I even suggested such an idea, and of course answered, "No."

"Well then," I continued, "what do you expect from your son? He comes home, opens his mouth and you fill it. You take care of his every need. Where should he learn that life isn't like that if you haven't taught him?"

Now, I am not suggesting, that we actually lock the door and let our kids sleep in the back yard. I am sure that comes close to child abuse. But what I am suggesting is that it isn't our children's fault if they are selfish. Generosity doesn't come naturally and it isn't learned from how generous you are to your children, it's learned more from how you treat your spouse.

We will discuss this more throughout the book, so please hold on.

The second point is, up until around eight years old, a child's identity is fused to that of the parent, so the child sees the parents pains or needs as his own. But as children grow and attain their own identity, separate from that of the parents, they don't feel the same need to attend to their parents wishes.

This all changes by the way, when the child becomes a parent. At that point the child gets an appreciation for what the parent did and can then identify, and is often genuinely grateful.

I often joke with my wife, although neither of us find it that funny: if the kids were to come home one day and see either of us in bed with tubes coming out of every place a tube could come out of, heart monitors beeping away and hoists and bandages of every description, they would take one look and then ask, "So, when will dinner be ready?"

The reason it isn't that funny, is we both know it's not too far from the truth.

But what's even more amazing is, parents don't mind. Somehow, when you have a baby the new parents get radiated and unbeknownst to them, that part of the parents brain that covers self-respect shrinks to non-existence.

My two year old son thinks nothing of giving me the contents of his nose, and in truth, it doesn't bother me that much either. Believe me, if anyone had tried to do that to me before I was married, we would have had serious problems.

THE SADDEST DAY

If you have children, then you should be able to answer this question: What is the worst thing your son/daughter could ever say to you?

No, it's not, "Hi Mom, I know you don't like me calling you at work, but I didn't want you to worry when you saw the house on the local TV news. I'm OK, and the science experiment I was working on went great, although I haven't seen the dog in a while."

The *real* answer is: "Don't help me anymore."

Strange as it seems, one of your parents saddest days was the day you moved out. Yes, I am sure it was bitter sweet, you have grown up (hopefully), but bitter in as much as parents need to give.

This is a universal truth: more than your children want to take, you as parents need to give. Parents often get stuck on this concept. They think that their children and they have an equal relationship. That their children want to please them as much as they want to please their children. Even if you know this is not the case, many parents will ask their children to be reciprocal in what they do for them. If this is not clear to you, all you need to think about is how little you "need" to make your parents happy when compared to what you want to do for your children. Well, your children have the same relationship to you as you do to your parents.

BEING NEEDED

How many times have you heard, or maybe even said yourself, "my kids need me!" I hear it all the time as the reason a parent has to sacrifice themselves for their children.

Not that there is really anything wrong with that sentiment, it's just that this same parent will also declare, "My spouse is driving me nuts, "he/she is soooo needy!"

The same quality (needy) makes a child endearing, even cute, but in a spouse becomes a source of endless frustration and tension.

Why?

This is an amazing story. I was once counseling a couple who were going through a rather difficult time in their marriage. To be quite honest, it wasn't going very well. Nothing I said seemed to help and things were deteriorating quickly.

Then one day, the wife (we will call her Tracy) called me to say her husband had taken ill and is going in for some rather serious surgery. I, of course, was concerned and even more, disappointed, "That's all this couple needed were more problems." I felt pretty sure this would kill off their relationship.

A little while went by and Tracy called me up for an appointment. She sounded terrible.

During the appointment Tracy explained how she couldn't take it anymore. I was waiting for her to tell me how much worse their relationship had become. I braced myself for the worst....

Was I surprised.

She did tell me how she felt her life had deteriorated drastically, her husband needed constant care, he was totally bedridden and she felt her life had degraded to that of an indentured slave.

She was miserable and told me so, although she didn't need to tell me, it was written all over her face.

I finally got up the courage to ask her <u>THE</u> question, "So how is your relationship with your husband?"

Tracy stopped and reflected for a few seconds, and then she said, "You know it's weird, but it hasn't been this good in years."

BEING NEEDED

Isn't it a great thing to be needed. It says we are important. Wouldn't it be a shame if we died and no one noticed?

I remember a song from the 70's about "People who need people, are the luckiest people in the world." The truth is, it's not "people who need people" it should rather say, "people who are needed by people" are the luckiest. Why do parents like being parents? Because they like being needed.

But, of all the people who need you the most, your spouse tops the list. Yet spouses are the people resented the most because, "My husband is soooo needy."

Adoption works because almost anyone can raise your children. Children are pretty much generic. They all need the same thing (we will talk more on this later). True, some kids have special needs, but you aren't especially qualified to satisfy those needs more than anyone else.

Put a different way, the problems we have with our children are not unique. Millions of people have the same problems. That is why there are generic books on dealing with the issues we have in parenting.

However, your spouse, as you have come to find out, is one of a kind.

You are in a very unique position. You are the only person who really knows your spouses issues – *and don't you know it!* You just don't know how to solve those issues, or maybe you don't think it's your job.

Bob Newhart remarks that his wife doesn't find him as funny as his audience because she knows what is really going on. This echoes an old Yiddish saying, there are only two people who know who you really are, G-d and your spouse. I would like to add to that, on the off-chance G-d hasn't told you what you are doing wrong, listen to your wife.

YOUR JOB

There is a tremendous misnomer about marriage that is not only wrong, but immensely detrimental. I hear it all the time, 'don't get married expecting your spouse to change.'

Let's start with something we can all agree upon, nobody is perfect. That being the case, it is just a matter of time till those little imperfections in your spouse start to drive you crazy. Therefore your job is to fix your spouse. Because people think they shouldn't expect their spouse to change, they think they have to find someone with no faults.

We need to think about this, unless of course you were perfect, why would someone who has no faults be interested in you?

We are not perfect and our spouses are not perfect, together we make our selves better. The mistake is thinking this will be easy.

Truth be told, by the time you are married you realize this is a daunting task, but that is hardly the point. Newborn babies are pitiful. They are unable to do the most basic of human activity on their own. And yet somehow after years and years of work they become people.

With parenting, we relish the challenge, we enjoy the process, we treasure the achievements along the road. Many people have scrap books collecting the exact date and time their progeny walked for the first time, or was toilet trained, maybe even their first word.

The same should be true with marriage. What was the day your husband/wife realized they are married. They thought of you, they apologized in a new way, they listened?

When it comes to our children we cherish those moments of breakthrough, with our spouses we often resent that their mother's didn't raise them properly and we had to do the dirty work.

I don't know about you, but there is nothing more dirty than changing a diaper, that's the dirty work. Making your spouse more perfect is a privilege.

If you know your spouse's issues, then you need to understand them. Once you understand them, you should be able to figure out how to solve them.

Why did Tracy's relationship improve? Because her husband needed her and she felt meaningful being needed.

I told her something very interesting. We all have choices in life and Tracy's was a choice between a comfortable life or a meaningful one. Sometimes you can have both, but that is rare. Usually you have to choose. Tracy was torn because she really wanted both and it wasn't going to happen.

"Tracy," I said, "you have a choice: a great marriage or an easy life – which one do you prefer?"

"Keep working on your relationship and things will only get better, and your life will be far more meaningful."

"Get a divorce, and your life will be far easier. You will have time to relax, catch a movie and take long bath's, but you will be alone doing it."

The truth is, we all make this choice when we have children. We end up with a far more meaningful life. But it isn't what I would call a great quality of life waking up in the middle of the night with a hysterical, vomiting child. Trying to calm him down and at the same time protect yourself from bodily fluids, may be interesting (in retrospect), but it isn't fun.

Sitting in the passenger seat trying to breathe slowly as my daughter takes the car out for the first time, is not what I would call a joy ride. But it does make the relationship work and your life more meaningful.

On the other hand, if you decide to not have the 'pain' of children, your life will be a lot easier, but maybe not as meaningful – it's your choice.

The same is true with a spouse (although hopefully you don't have to worry about the vomit – I can't say the same about the joy ride.) By identifying your spouse's needs as real and urgent, you have found someone to give to, and your life, as Tracy found out, becomes richer for it.

Tracy, (before her husband's medical crisis) wanted an easy care-free life. Her husband's needs were viewed by her as irritants that were becoming increasingly annoying (as were her needs to her husband). When the medical crisis hit, she saw his needs in an altogether different light and felt an obligation to help.

We do this naturally with our children. We even do it at our jobs. And we feel good when we do it. It's amazing how much pride a person feels after years of building up a business, even though it's been an excruciatingly painful process of dealing with pain-in-the-neck customers.

Most spouses are nowhere near as difficult as your customers, your boss or probably your co-workers. So, if we can be in the "I want to help" mode at work or with our children, can't we do the same with our spouse?

A SLIGHT DIGRESSION

In the early 1950's Roger Banister announced to the world that he would run the mile in under four minutes.

Everyone thought it was impossible. The sports "experts," the medical establishment, everyone.

In 1954 he did it.

Within one year there were people running faster than Banister himself.

When asked how was it possible for so many people to run that fast so soon after everyone said it was impossible, Banister responded: 'it was never a physical barrier, it was a mental barrier.'

The Talmud tells a very similar story. When we meet God in the next world, the Almighty will ask each one of us why we didn't achieve more in life.

The Talmud tells us that each of us will come with a different excuse.

However, God pulls out someone with that very same excuse and nevertheless was able to achieve that which we were not.

Now, God will ask again, "How come they had the same handicap, yet it didn't stop them?"

How embarrassing!

I would like to ask a question, why does God need to present anyone? God knows us, and knows that we could have done it?

Why didn't God say something like, "Oh grow up and stop whining you wimp – we both know you could have done it."

The same question could be asked about those other runners – why couldn't they do it before 1954?

Because they didn't think they could do it till they saw Roger Banister do it.

_WE_ need to know **_WE_** can do it!

It isn't enough that God knows, we need to know. When we see someone else achieve something, then we know we can do it too.

That is part of what it means, "We are all created equal." If I am the same as you, then I should be able to do what you can do.

But, Roger Banister is telling us something even deeper, **listen up people:**

>*"We will only strive for something we think we can achieve."*

You don't know what you can do till you see someone else do it.

So (big drum role here....) THE question is, how did Roger Banister know he could do it?

He didn't have the advantage of seeing anyone else do it?

The answer is, because God doesn't send you a problem you cannot overcome!

When you are faced with a problem, you **can** overcome it.

As long as you don't give up, you will succeed. If you don't give up, you will solve your spouses problems.

I am sure you have had this experience. You and a friend are looking at exactly the same scene, yet, you see it as an obstacle to overcome, and your friend sees it as a brick wall, and gives up.

If you are faced with a problem, it means you can solve it.

I once saw this quote, which in and of itself is remarkable, but is even more powerful when you see who said it:

"Giving up is the final solution to a temporary problem." Anonymous Holocaust Survivor.

LAME EXCUSES

Many people today don't believe it is possible to achieve Bliss in marriage, so they don't try. They see marriage as a brick wall and give up.

We all have our excuse. We say: "it's not my fault, *I'm not getting anything out of this relationship anymore!*"

The first step to making your marriage blissful, is to realize *"I'm not getting anything out of this relationship anymore!"* is a very, very lame excuse.

Since when did you get anything out of your relationship with your child?

"How did you manage to love, care and give so much to your children when they gave you so little?" For sure, your children give love, but in terms of making your life easier, they don't come close to what your spouse does for you.

If "not getting anything out of this relationship" is not relevant when it comes to your children, can't you be the same with your spouse?

EINSTEIN

A joke is told that Einstein meets an actress. The actress says, "Let's have children together. Just think – your brains and my looks."

Einstein retorts back to her, "But what if they have my looks and your brains!?"

What I am going to show you is that all the great techniques of marriage are well known to you, and not only that, but you employ them extremely successfully....

With your children!

In other words, you are a great spouse with your kids.

Not only that, but we also have all the techniques we need to be the best parent, we just use them with our spouse.

It's the wrong looks with the wrong brains!

In other words, we aren't going to learn any new techniques in this book. You won't have to apply any new rigorous methods and strategies. You know everything you need and apply them well, just in the wrong places.

You know what to do and can do it well, you just need to change who you do it with and you can be that great parent, and you can achieve that marital bliss.

You already have done all the work, acquired all the skills, it's now time to employ them with the right people.

Chapter 1:
<u>You Could Have Done Better!</u>

SCENE: An expensive downtown florist.

In walks a man who laboriously deliberates every detail of a bouquet.

After 45 minutes, painstakingly assembling a most remarkable and appropriately expensive assembly of exotic flowers, the florist rings up the quite impressive bill, she remarks: "A surprise for your wife?"

"Yes...." He answers, "She's expecting diamonds!"

Nothing in life is ever what it really is; it's only relative to what you expect it to be.

Put in the right context the gym will make your day, but not when you were expecting a relaxing date with your spouse. If your spouse calls you up to tell you we are going out for dinner and you were expecting French cuisine but get Fast-Food, it will ruin your evening, but the other way around will make your week.

With this in mind, rarely, did anyone ever marry a disaster, what they married is less than they expected.

How much less?

Let's put it this way, if you married Prince Charming who woke every morning to greet you with breakfast in bed. Whose only dream, all day long was to fulfill your every whim, and only went to sleep after your extensive to-do list was accomplished in full. Who never complained and loved having your mother over, still you would say, "I could have done better!"

I know you are all saying, "no I wouldn't!"

All I can say is, it isn't going to happen, so let's not debate it.

But, more importantly, no one married such a person. I mean ever. In other words, everyone thinks they could have done better.

We have all been raised on ridiculous fairy tales of Snow White and Cinderella. We all expect to meet Prince Charming and live happily ever after.

I want you to repeat after me, **"THERE IS NO SUCH THING!"**

That's why they are fairy tales, they are fiction.

People have forgotten the definition of fiction.

The definition of fiction: what to read when you can't take reality anymore. In other words, reality is too tough, so writers created a different ending. Wake up people, "Sleeping Beauty" is not auto-biographical!

Just like you go to college and the real hard work begins when you get a job. And just like you have a baby, and the real hard work begins when you bring the baby home. So too, when you put that ring on your finger, the really hard work begins. Anyone who thinks that all you have to do is lie down half-dead (as in Snow White) and wait for a noble prince to show up to kiss you, wake up and walk off together into the sunset to spend the rest of your life in dream-like-bliss, is working for Disney.

NUTS

The reason marriage never meets our expectations, is that our expectations are not just extreme, they are off-the-deep-end nuts.

Now a lot of people get confused with this point. They think it means that you should live with whatever your spouse dishes out. They think it means that giving up your expectations is akin to letting your spouse get away with murder.

This is not true, anymore than you live with what your children dish out.

The difference is, and it's a huge difference, when your children ruin your new couch or scratch your new car, you are probably going to be upset with them (to say the least) but you won't be disappointed. You won't be thinking, this is not what I expected or bargained for.

Or, put another way, if you call up your mother to tell her what trouble your little Johnny got into today, your mother won't suggest an adoption agency.

But, call up your mother about something your husband did (I would not suggest doing this) and your mother will not only give you the number of three divorce lawyers, but will no doubt add the line: "I always knew he was no good for you, but I didn't want to say anything."

Now imagine your mother called you and said, "Darling, Mrs. Jones next door just put her little Johnny up for adoption, and I have never seen her happier."

A few more phone calls like that, and you won't be speaking to your mother.

The point is, get used to the fact marriage is no picnic, and when it comes to parenting, you probably are used to it.

When it comes to children, when they ruin your day, you are upset but not terribly surprised. You didn't expect NOT to have some disaster (or 15 disasters) happen to you over the course of your parenting career.

Similarly, it doesn't mean you can't be upset with your spouse about letting you down or not doing something they were supposed to do. But, the point is, if your child were to let you down, you wouldn't say (even to yourself, let alone to your mother) I think they switched babies on us at the hospital.

But when your spouse does something upsetting, you will probably mutter, "Mom was right, he is a loser."

A spouse is no more a loser than your child could be a loser. I am sure it happens, but I have never heard of such a thing, that a parent thinks of his/her child as a loser. No mother ever said to me, "My son, the loser." Well, that spouse of yours is someone's child.

Your spouse isn't a loser, it's you. **You gave up!**

In the same way, if you ever meet a parent that thinks of their child as a loser, it's not the child's fault, but rather it's the parent to blame, similarly, it's not the spouse that's the loser, it's you.

Maybe I am not being clear here, so let me say it another way. If you find yourself thinking you could have done better, that maybe you were too hasty in marrying, that the next one will be more what you need, then tattoo this on your forehead:

I am an idiot!

Your spouse has nothing to do with you being upset – true, they may be in the wrong, but that in no way justifies your extreme feelings. Your feelings would never be so deep if it were your child and in many cases, they wouldn't be that bad if it were your dog.

I can't tell you how many times people with dogs tell me horror stories of what their dog did in the kitchen. I don't have a dog, but often when I hear one of these stories I think to myself, "What if your husband did that in the kitchen, would you be so forgiving?"

I know you expect more from your husband (I hope). But, what it should demonstrate to you is, it's not the crime that got you upset (in this case spoiling a perfectly nice carpet), it's the expectations surrounding the perpetrator.

Your feelings are bent out of shape because your expectations were unrealistic.

Picture this scene:

It's the so called family vacation. Kids screaming in the back of the car, parents popping aspirin like crazy, constant bickering and of course the ubiquitous line: "are we there yet?"

And yet, at the end of the trip, your eight year old daughter comes over to you and gives you a hug and a little kiss on the cheek and says, "Thank you Daddy, for a great vacation."

Your heart melts and you turn to your wife and say, "that was the best vacation, we should do this more often."

Alternatively, you take two weeks, just you and your spouse to some exclusive Caribbean island where you are fanned on the beaches drinking pina colada's. Every meal is as though it were taken out of a gourmet magazine, and the entertainment is as good as anything on Broadway – it's the dream vacation.

However, on the way back you get into a viscous argument with your spouse over who gets the aisle seat, and in a moment of rage, you turn to your spouse and shout: "I wish I had never gone, I should have stayed at the office!"

And you mean it. And your spouse agrees.

Why do we have such a different reaction to our family vacation than that of a vacation with just the two of you?

Expectations.

It's like buying a very, very expensive car; the smallest problem will ruin your day. You expected it to be perfect. You will spend hours on the phone complaining to customer relations how the ash-tray doesn't work properly (even though you don't smoke). However, if you buy a 15 year old wreck, you feel grateful that most of the wheels go round.

When you buy a cheap junk car, you would like everything to work. But, when the window handle falls off, you try and figure out how to fix it and you don't really spend any time complaining about it.

But, when the heater stops working in the new Rolls Royce, you won't fix it. You won't even try, even though with the amount of time you will spend complaining is more than enough to take apart the whole engine and put it back together again.

With the Rolls, there is an expectation that it should be 100% perfect. With the cheap car, you understand you bought the problems.

The same is true with marriage. We think we shouldn't have problems. However, you should not think you bought a piece of junk, it's just that you bought into something that is going to be a challenge. Just like work, just like exercise.

Just like kids.

SUMMARY

With this idea in hand I am sure you can realize by now what a dramatic effect it will have on your marriage, if you take it seriously.

In sum, all your frustrations, disappointments, grudges and issues you have with your spouse that contribute to the feeling that you don't have a blissful marriage have nothing to do with your spouse -- nothing!

But they have everything to do with you.

I can hear every person who has made it to this point in the book scream and throw something in my direction.

So, I want to re-emphasize the point, it doesn't mean your wife/husband is right. It means that his issues are your challenges. **A challenge is not a disappointment.**

Imagine showing up on the first day of your new job after graduating from school and your new boss lays out all the challenges and problems she wants you to solve and overcome.

How ridiculous would it be to say, "I didn't bargain for this; I thought after school it was clear sailing -- I just show up and you just mail the check!"

Work is a challenge. It is difficult, painful, and sometimes disturbing, but it is not a disappointment.

Marriage is the same. It is difficult, painful, and sometimes disturbing, but it is not a disappointment. Your husbands issues are your challenges. Your wifes' idiosyncrasies are your goals. You have to figure out how to deal and work with them to achieve harmony.

That's your job, enjoy it, take pride in it, and for sure, don't be disappointed in it.

Chapter 2:
<u>1st Class Parents</u>

50% of all marriages end in divorce.

**That
does not
mean
the
other
50%
are living
in Bliss!**

There are two types of light switches, the simple kind, the ones that give you a choice of on or off. And then there are the ones that make you think, they usually have a dial or bar that can set the lighting to any brightness you want.

When I was a kid I was only exposed to the first kind of switches, and therefore, for me, the lights were either on or off. But with these more sophisticated switches, it is not exact to say that the lights are either on or off, we need more words to describe the situation.

Similarly, many people tend to think, there are only two types of marriages, those that end in divorce and those in bliss. On or off.

Now for sure, some marriages are off and in divorce. But few are fully "on." Meaning, few marriages could be described as bliss. For most the lights are on, but they are way too dim to get around without stubbing your toe on the furniture.

Thinking that marriages are either on or off makes you think that the secret to a happy marriage is endurance --- if we aren't divorced we must be in the "on" position, i.e. we must get to bliss. Marriage is not the Tour de France. Endurance may help you to not get divorced but it won't give you bliss, just a lot of heart burn.

I like to compare Marriage to going to the dentist. The fact that you don't use Novocain, doesn't mean it doesn't hurt, it just means your tolerance for pain is very high.

People who don't get divorced are not necessarily less miserable than those who do get divorced – they just have a higher tolerance for misery.

WHAT A DIFFERENCE A DAY MAKES

Remember when you first met your future spouse? I am sure you remember all kinds of seemingly irrelevant details, what you were wearing, the weather, décor, etc,. The day you met the world stood still, he's your prince in shining armor and you couldn't be happier if you tried. Wild horses couldn't drag the smiles off your faces.

Then on a different day, somewhere in-between the wedding day and your two year anniversary, the dream disappeared and "reality" set in.

For some it's sheer misery, for others it's reasonable boredom, they might even find it a little pleasant.

But bliss it ain't!

A lot of people I meet have given up the dream of living in bliss with their spouse. They have settled, and made peace with the idea this is as good as it is ever going to get.

Often they live vicariously through their children. They promise themselves that their children will live a better life. Their children will not make the same mistakes they made. They settle for martyrdom, they become secret heroes, somehow convincing themselves that their sacrifice is for the greater good and one day their children will erect a statue in their honor.

If you are one of these people, you are in for a big surprise.

These so called heroes reason, "I blew it, but my children will rise from the ashes of my mistakes and so my life will not be in vain." If the hero married young, they tell their children to wait. If they married a doctor, they will tell their children to marry a lawyer."

These people think the secret to bliss is to not make the mistakes they have made.

This advice doesn't help because it isn't your dream you want your children to live, it is only your nightmare you are trying to avoid.

It's sort of like investing all your money in a stock you pick at random because your father lost all his money in bonds.

This is reminiscent of a joke:

> A young man brings home a women to meet his mother. And even though he is very excited about her, the boy's mother tells him, "she isn't for you – too short."
>
> OK, he keeps looking and brings home a tall woman, only to be rebuffed again by his mother, "No, not for you, she's a blonde."
>
> This goes on many times, finally he finds a woman that is just like his mother in every way possible.

He brings her home and the mother immediately opens her heart and applauds her son on his great choice.

All is good however, until he introduces her to his father who can't stand her!

THE GREATEST PLEASURE

If you ask the average person, "What is your greatest pleasure in life?" Most will answer, their children.

Now ask them this, "What should be your greatest pleasure?"

One of the wisest men alive today, Rabbi Noah Weinberg points out, "What people should say is, their greatest pleasure is their spouse."

If you think about it, this is obvious. Everyone wants their children to marry someone who is the love of their lives. Could you imagine walking your daughter down the aisle, to be shocked when she tells you, "Mom/dad – I really don't like him that much!"

What will you answer, "That's OK dear, we don't like each other that much either, but we had children."

We all want our children to marry the love of their lives, someone who they will hold hands in glowing admiration of each other as they walk the beach of life into the sunset.

We don't want our children to marry someone who they can only tolerate because they have kids!

The problem is, if 50% of marriages end in divorce, and most of the 50% who stay married are far from bliss, who is going to teach your children how to be happily married, if not you?

GIVE YOUR CHILDREN THE BEST

We spend fortunes in money and time to make sure our children get the best education we can find. After all, we don't want our children to suffer the pain and humiliation of struggling to earn a living. Yet, if you have ever experienced the pain of divorce or custody battles, the pain of poverty pales.

Yet we pay scant attention to ensure our children know how to make marriage work.

To be honest, I don't understand why the basic ideas of marriage and parenting are not taught in schools. Divorce is the single largest known factor causing poverty in America today. It diminishes assets and destroys productivity. The country spends vast fortunes on the ill effects that broken homes inflict on children. Yet, kids today don't even get a book on how to be happily married.

If children have to learn history and geography, subjects far more abstract than communication and tolerance, yet the need for these subjects is far more necessary, why isn't it in every schools' curriculum?

But the purpose of this book is not solely to berate the education policy of this country, it's to get you, as parents to realize:

You can't raise first rate children, with a second rate marriage.

If you are not teaching your children how to make marriage work, then you are setting them up for a life of pain and misery.

In other words, if you want to give your children the best life can offer, give them a happy marriage – yours.

Chapter 3:
MarPar

At its essence, the ideas I am presenting, are that parenting teaches you how to be a better spouse, and marriage teaches you how to be a better parent.

If you read the previous paragraph too quickly you probably missed the point I am trying to make, one that will change everything you do and how you think of yourself. Parenting not marriage, teaches you how to have a great marriage. Marriage, not parenting, teaches you how to be a great parent.

I like to call it the MARPAR concept (MAR marriage PAR parenting).

Marpar goes like this: you already possess all the skills and ability to become a great spouse, and you are practicing them..... with your children. And if you don't have children, you hopefully can see that others who have similar marital issues as you do practice them with their children. You can do the same.

And the reverse is also true. The skills you need to become a better parent are to be found in your role as a spouse. People are great parents with their spouses, and great spouses with their children.

We are going to go through five examples, although I am sure there are more, and as you understand the concept better you will be able to find others yourself:

1) Quality Time vs. Quantity Time
2) Give and Take
3) Survival vs. Success
4) Technique vs. Caring
5) Forgive and Forget

Chapter 4:
<u>QUALITY TIME vs.</u>
<u>QUANTITY TIME</u>

E may equal MC², but no amount of quality time will equal any amount of quantity time to a four year old.

In fact, children operate on a sliding scale, the older the child, the less they want quality time and more they need quantity time. Or, put differently, the more they grow closer to you in intellectual proficiencies, the less they want to talk to you.

I know, it's a tough wrap, your children are never going to want you for anything deeper than Barney or the Teletubbies. In other words, your children will love you for playing Thomas the Train and Lego, but forget about the meaning of life.

Or, put another way, if you are looking for intellectual adult stimulation – talk to your spouse.

The sliding rule is not an absolute and there are exceptions, it's a variable depending on the child. But for the most part, there is a base line of 80/20. 80% of the time is quantity and 20% is quality.

Children don't want quality time, they want quantity time. Children don't want to talk to you (quality), but they do want you around (quantity).

Of all the time you spend with your children, 80% should be quantity time and 20% quality. 20% is a lot and they need that too, and in fact, the younger the child the higher the ratio. In other words, under eight years old, a child needs a lot more than 20% quality time. But as children grow they appreciate more the quantity time than the quality.

Quantity time tells your children you care about them, and this is one of the most important messages your children need to hear.

But, if you are not giving the quality time and think you are doing fine by giving a lot of quantity time instead, it will show. Just as if you are missing a needed vitamin in your system, you won't look too good.

It's important to appreciate the friction that comes from children when we overdose them on quality time.

I am always amused by the first day of school. My job as a parent is to do the due diligence and ask my children how it went. There is always one of my children who will answer honestly, "It was boring," or some similar response.

With that, I leap into my "Even if it's boring you can still learn from all teachers" lecture. All my other children roll their eyes and make sure no one answers the question that way again. Sometimes force is exerted.

My children could have had a Marine Drill Sergeant run the school that day and they would still come home and tell me how much they enjoyed school. Not because they did, but because they don't really want to talk to me.

I try not to take it personally.

As Tony Kornheiser once told me, "Children will give you the least possible answer, for the least possible response."

They don't want to talk to me, but they do want me around. They like me being in the house or driving them places. They like me sitting with them and they love me watching them skate or play, but they hate it when I try and dialogue with them.

Parents are often aghast at this point, "What do you mean my children don't want to communicate with me?"

Do children need to talk out issues with you? For sure, you need to be there for them. And that is the operative function here, you have to be there. When they are ready they will come to you and talk or ask. Don't push yourself into your child's life where you are not totally welcome or you will find that you are spending less than 20% in quality time.

Your child will push you away. This is a fine balance, you need to be interested in your child's life and you need to show you are interested. But they also need a private life, separate from you. The balance is to be found in your motive.

Do you like having your parents around, probably yes? Does it get on your nerves when they pry into your life? Probably yes.

Realize, that your children view you the same way you view your parents.

The other extreme is also bad, less than 20% quality time can have disastrous results. Be involved in their lives, know what they are up to. Just keep it to 20%.

THE MIRROR

What is interesting, is that with marriage it's the opposite.

A spouse needs QUALITY TIME.

You could spend a whole weekend away, alone on a deserted island just you and your wife, the vacation from paradise – very similar to the Caribbean trip above, but better. Then, on the way back your wife will tell you, "You know, we never get time to talk!"

You did a lot of things together, but you didn't talk, you didn't really communicate.

Quality time, not quantity time is the key. Half an hour is all it takes. Just a few minutes of focused communication between you and your spouse on the things that count will make your spouses' day.

Conversation (not chatter): "How are you really feeling?" "What happened to you today?" What are your thoughts?" etc. This means the world to a spouse and a relationship.

Now isn't it interesting that we feel comfortable sitting at the breakfast table reading the paper right in front of our spouse, yet we can't sit quiet for a moment without barraging our kids with 20 questions at every opportunity we get.

MARPAR: We know how to do it, we just need to switch.

Be interested in your spouses life, like you are with your children's. Be comfortable just relaxing with your kids like you are with your spouse.

BAD EXCUSES

Did you ever come home tired from a day at the office and your spouse wanted to talk?

Have you ever responded with, "Honey, you know I would love to talk, but I am zonked, lets get together over the weekend."

But if on that same evening, your teenage son comes into your bedroom just as you were about to nod off and says, "Dad, I just read this book on the meaning of life, and I just don't understand what my purpose is?"

You would be dressed and ready quicker than you can say, "blue moon." You would be focused and ready to discuss the intricacies of existential philosophy till the early hours of the morning.

Why?

With our kids, we want a relationship.

Let me repeat that because it is THE key to a great relationship. We want a relationship with our children so we work on it, hard, often and always.

Get it?

If you want it, it will happen. That is the spice of the relationship – that is why dating was so exciting.

You wanted the relationship, you wanted to explore each other to find out as much as you could.

You haven't changed, you still want a relationship – you have to want it with your spouse. You can do it, you just have to try.

Now, if you are finding yourself asking, "How do I develop this relationship with my spouse?" you missed the whole point (sorry).

Did you need a manual when you were dating? The reason there aren't "Dating Counselors" is because when people really want to understand each other, they will find a way.

"Yes." You tell me. "But what if I want to understand and be interested in my spouse, but my spouse isn't that interested in me?"

I get this question a lot.

Have you ever seen anyone with a crush? Does it matter if they are ignored by the crushee?

More than that, unless you are married to someone in deep freeze, your spouse will notice you being elated and excited to be around them. Because of your interest and concern for them, and them alone, it will slowly, slowly engender an interest and concern back.

Have patience and keep practicing.

Chapter 5:
Give and Take

JOKE: When it comes to my children,
there are only two things I worry
about.

One is, that when they grow up,
they won't be able to manage
without me.

The other thing I worry about is,
maybe they will.

Once, while in Israel I visited a dairy farm with some
friends. It was during calving season, so the farm
was a bustle with baby cows, calves to be precise.
It was all very cute.

However, we were all bothered by the fact that the
new calves were not suckling from their mothers, as
we had seen in the movies, but rather from farm
hands with bottles. Baby bottles to be precise.

It was a little surreal. Instead of what one would
normally expect to be at the other end of a baby
bottle, as we had seen in real life, people were
walking around with 20 pound calves.

Upon inquiry, we were informed, they take the calf away from the mother immediately at birth. Since the mother only produces as much milk as the calf takes, if they wait until the calf has properly weaned away from the mother cow, then the mother is useless as a milk cow.

Wow, what they don't teach you in high school.

So, we asked, why at birth? Why not wait a few days before you take the calf away? At least they could get a little acquainted. To take the calf away at birth seems so cruel.

They told us that they once did that. They let a calf stay with its mother for longer, and when they finally took it away, the mother cried.

I have never heard a cow cry. Now and again, when driving through the country I will see a cow in a field and I am always tempted to run over to it and whisper in it's ear: "Hey, you are really ugly!" and see what happens. But I don't have the heart. However, I am told that the cry of the cow is so mournful and incessant you can't sleep at night.

They told us at the dairy farm that the mother, the one whom they left the calf with, cried for days and days when they finally took the calf away.

I learned a very important principle from that story. If you had asked the average guy, "Who do you think is more likely to cry, the mother or the calf?" I believe most would reason that the calf was more likely of the two. For very obvious reasons, the calf is the one who seems to be losing the most.

From the fact that the calf doesn't cry, but the mother does, we conclude the opposite, it's the mother that must be losing the most – but what?

The Talmud gives us the answer: "More than the calf wants to take, the cow needs to give."

Remember what we said above, the worst thing your children can say to you is "don't help me anymore."

I remember a mother calling me up extremely distraught. No, not the cow at the dairy farm – I'm a Rabbi not an animal psychiatrist.

Anyway, she (the human mother) was very sweet but was bothered that her daughter didn't call her enough or change her plans to fit in with her mother's life style.

I told the mother, listen, there is a fact of life going on here. "You need your children more than they need you."

There was a moment of silence, a long moment. She was incredulous; this just can't be true.

So I asked her, was *her* mother still alive? "Yes."
How often do you call your mother and how much
do you "need" to see her.

The penny dropped.

She hung up the phone as though she was looking
from the crows nest of the Mayflower and had just
shouted down to the crew, "end of the world in
sight!"

She called me back a few weeks later. She needed
that amount of time to digest what I told her. She
told me how much she appreciated the insight and
how it helped in her relationship with her daughter.
Once she understood the rules of the game, it all fit
and made sense.

GIVE OR TAKE

With our children, there is no "give and take," there
is only give.

Not only is it all give, we wouldn't want it any other
way. What kind of meaningful relationship could we
possibly have with our children if we billed them
each week?

A parent looks forward to a son visiting home and
takes pride in doing his laundry.

If you have a healthy relationship with your parents, you know how happy it makes them when they make you dinner. In fact, you will make your father's day if you call him up and ask for his advice.

Do you realize what this would mean if you could relate to your spouse that way? Does it bother you when your wife asks for help? Does it drive you crazy when your husband asks you where something is? Does it make your day to do dinner, laundry, errands for each other?

Think I am going a little too far?

Visit a couple that had trouble getting pregnant and after 10 years finally had a baby. You never saw joy like the joy on a mother's face as she changes the baby's diaper.

Do you realize what she is doing?

Before I got married one of my Rabbis, a real genius in human relations: Rabbi Zelig Pliskin told me, "marriage is not give and take, it's all give."

When it comes to children, you aren't waiting to get anything back – and if you are, don't hold your breath.

But with marriage, unfortunately, many people expect something back. We keep a tally of what we have done for our spouse, and what our spouse has done for us, and we expect it to be even or close.

"I did the dishes, that's equal to taking out the garbage twice."

The bottom line: "Give and Take" is not give at all, it's just a nicer way of saying take.

It's no more than a glorified maid. I pay the maid to make dinner. If I pay my wife to do it by doing something for her, what's the difference?

None.

The truth is, if we could get away with it, we would rather not pay the maid. In other words, if we could get her to do the floors for nothing, great. And if we could get our spouses to do what we want them to do, without any quid-pro-quo, fantastic.

That's not a relationship, that's self gratification. I don't care about my spouse, I only care about me.

Unfortunately many people, if not the vast majority get married thinking that is what is going to happen....are they surprised.

In a similar way people will claim they love a particular type of food. "I love steak." But is that what you do to something you love? You eat it?

No, you don't love steak, you love yourself and you love what the steak does for you.

If you "love" your spouse for what they do for you, you don't love your spouse, you love you!

Bliss is different. The reason you get such bliss from your children is you don't expect anything back. Your pleasure is in seeing your kids happy. That's your payback. Because you care about your children.

If you are into "give and take" with your spouse, it's because you just don't care about her!

That's not an excuse, it's a beginning. Start caring.

How do you do that?

Give without any expectation of anything back.

I know it's difficult, but you can do it. You just have to practice.

Your child came into this world with far less virtues than your spouse and gave you far greater headaches, and yet, despite this you poured your heart and soul into doing everything you could to make that precious little child as happy as could be. And because of that you loved them.

You didn't love them and then sacrificed, you sacrificed and that made you love them. A lot of mothers tell me, as soon as the baby was born they loved them, unconditionally and without end. I am sure this is true, but it was only after nine months of having your bladder squeezed and being kicked from the inside. In other words, by the time the doctor slapped that baby on the rear-end, you had paid big time in sweat and tears – you were deeply invested in that child.

If you treat your marriage the same way, you will have bliss. This doesn't mean put up with abuse. Don't be an idiot, don't be taken advantage. It means look at your husband/wife and ask, "What is the most I can do to make this person the best person they can possible be?"

If you have children, you will already be familiar with that question, now use it on your spouse.

WHY DO PEOPLE WANT TO HAVE CHILDREN?

Everyone who has children tells everyone else, the pleasure is phenomenal, and they trust that it will happen to them too.

You may think that there is incredible pleasure waiting for you when you have children, and you are right. But that is nothing compared to what you can have with your spouse.

Your marriage contains more bliss than you have with your children.

Hard to imagine?

If it wasn't for the fact that you know seemingly rational people that turn their lives upside down and lose all sense of civilized existence, because, as they tell you, "children are an incredible pleasure," you would never believe having children would improve the quality of life. We see so many people having children that we figure there has to be something in it. And there is.

But it is hard to explain to a single person the joy of children, when everything a single person has come to appreciate will pretty much disappear after kids. Marriage is the same. After you put in the effort to make your marriage great, you won't be able to explain the bliss you will experience.

The state of the world today, is such, that many mistakenly believe children are a greater pleasure than a spouse. If you will allow me, I will show you how incorrect that is.

It was not that long ago that you would not have understood the previous paragraph. You would have known without any doubt that marriage is more meaningful than parenting. That was when you were single. Single people on the whole are wholly convinced that nothing will outshine their spouse, and they should be right. Yet by the time they have children, generally speaking, they have completely forgotten that conviction.

How odd.

They forgot because they entered marriage with give and take and they didn't get the bliss they expected.

How much more meaningful marriage should and must be. How can a child, which is a one-way-street relationship compare to a spouse who shares your life, soul dreams, secrets, everything; how can a child be at all as great and as meaningful to that of a spouse?

It can't, unless you are not dedicated to your spouse as much as you are to your children.

A child will never care for you like your spouse will or can, they will never return the love like a spouse is able. Marriage is a two-way-street, the love goes both ways. How much more meaningful must that be.

One day, your kids will move out, and as you hold hands on that long beach called "the rest of your life," you don't want the tide of petty squabbles to wade in, and be eaten by the sharks of constant personal attacks.

If you want it to be a picture perfect scenario, you need to work on it now. The movie isn't over, but the actors are on the stage, and the plot is starting the thicken.

Have courage, be a hero, go for the bliss!

Chapter 6:
Survival vs. Success

Rabbi Yaacov Weinberg T'zl was a phenomenal teacher. He used to give a parable. Imagine walking into a hospital and meeting a surgeon. The surgeon asks the nature of the problem. You show him your finger and explain that you want him to cut it off.

Aghast, he asks what kind of treatment have you done?

"None, it's just been very painful lately."

For sure this is insane, but the message is very poignant. Before resorting to amputation, every other possible rock would have to be overturned. Amputation is only a consideration after trying everything else and the doctors inform you that if they don't amputate, you could lose your whole hand.

This is what I call a "success" relationship. A success relationship, is one where the problem HAS TO be solved. That's the kind of relationship you have with your hand. It's not that you wouldn't amputate, it's just not in your consciousness to even think about it until there is nothing left to do. You do not contemplate anything other than success.

That's the kind of relationship we have with our children. We are in success mode.

How many times have we met someone, a regular normal person, and as they talk, you find that they are one of the leading authorities on East African Whooping Cough, or some other exotic disease?

How come they know so much?

Their daughter caught it.

They have read *all* the studies. They have spoken to the leading doctors on the issue and even started a web-site. Even lobbied Congress.

With our children, we are in success mode.

What's the other mode?

Survival Mode.

This is what we typically have with our spouses.

Survival mode goes like this, if it's killing me then I will live with it.

When I confront people with why they didn't solve a problem in their marriage, people will often say: "I tried."

What does that mean?

It means I told him to grow up and he wouldn't listen.

"Did you say it like that?"

"No, of course not."

"I said, grow up you idiot!"

"It's not my fault he won't change. As I said, I tried."

And they mean it.

Did they read a book on communicating with their spouses?

Is there such a book: "How to Talk so Your Husband will Listen"?

Isn't it interesting, we live in a society where you can find a book on almost every kind of communication issue with your child, yet for your husband the only ideas you might hear for better dialogue is in The Muppets.

"I DIDN'T ASK FOR THIS!"

Did you ever hear that line?

With a spouse who gets ill, watches too much sports, loses his hair, puts on weight – yes.

But when it comes to a child, the biggest problem is viewed as part of the package. It's a problem you have to deal with. With marriage, problems are an "added benefit."

With Marriage, when our spouses develop an issue, why isn't the first question we ask: "How do I solve this?" In fact, that usually doesn't even come to mind. We have often given up changing our spouses.

The first question we ask is, "Can I live with this?"

With marriage, we are willing to live with anything less than a psychotic (some people live with even that.)

With parenting, our children develop the smallest problem and we don't sleep till it's resolved.

You probably know 2-5 pediatricians if needed, and very likely know an expert child therapist -- but wouldn't know where to begin in finding a marriage counselor.

The Yellow Pages?

Wrong.

How do you find the best pediatrician in town?

Yellow Pages?

I said the best, not any.

To find the best, you have to ask around, do some research, the same for finding a good marriage counselor. You don't want to waste your time seeing someone who doesn't know what they are talking about.

Not only that. Have you ever been to a pediatrician who didn't give you the answers you were looking for? She seemed too distracted or didn't seem to understand the symptoms? I can't tell you how many people stay with the same marriage counselor even though they know it's not going well.

We know how to get our car fixed better than we know how to fix our marriage.

How many times have I heard, "But my husband won't talk about it," "He refuses to dialogue with me on it," "When I bring it up with my wife, she has a fit!"

True, but compared to teenagers (boys especially) the communicative skills of your husband/wife, put Shakespeare to shame.

Since when has your child's willingness to reason stopped you from solving the problem. So if your son won't discuss it, you figure out how to work around him, you talk to his friends, plead with his teachers, anything.

I once got a phone call from the wife of a friend of mine. She wanted me to discuss an issue with her husband, and she even told me what she wanted the conclusion to be.

I asked her, "you know, you will see him before me?"

"Yes," she said, "but he will listen to you, there is only so much a spouse can do."

Hmmm, I thought, very devious. Clever, but devious.

Then I thought, I wonder how many times my wife has done that to me?"

I was going to ask her, but then I thought, why? If it works, great.

Believe me, if you were half as determined to solve your spouses problems as you were your children's,

you would be in more bliss than is legally allowed
behind a steering wheel.

Can you handle that much happiness?

Chapter 7:
Technique vs. Caring

Raising children is one of the easiest jobs you will ever undertake.

Unless of course, you want to get it right.

And-here-in lies the secret of parenting.

I have found that nobody has a clue how to raise children. When I say "nobody" I don't mean lay people, I don't mean plumbers, lawyers and CIA informants, I mean nobody. Including all the experts in parenting.

Of course anyone who has children knows this. To quote the famous Eddie Cantor, "Before I had children I had six theories on parenting, after six children I have none."

It's all a shot in the dark. Yes, true, we have experts that tell us to nurse babies and discipline with time-outs, etc., etc. But these are all general principles. When you get down to the specifics, it's all a guess. Is it better to nurse a child and ignore their older sibling, or give the baby a bottle for a change so you can have a good nights sleep and be able to give your children the attention they need tomorrow? How long should a time-out be? In all these decisions we can make educated guesses, but guesses all the same.

When there is a specific incident for which I need to discipline my children, I wonder, "did it scar them for life?" Or, I think, maybe the discipline wasn't strong enough and they therefore did not learn the lesson and will never get out of their bad habits?

When I reward them, did I make it challenging enough or too easy, and will that cripple them for the outside world where rewards are not so easily achieved?

Only on television can you sit down with your son after they hit their little sister and have a discussion about how to treat people, and the son "gets it." In real life, when you scold your children they will tell you (or let you know in other ways) that you are ruining them for life (mine do). Even when they tell you they understand, do they mean it?

Didn't you ever tell your parents what they wanted to hear? How difficult do you think it is for your children to figure that one out?

So when I say, nobody knows how to raise children, I mean nobody.

I know what I am doing when I change the oil in my car; I know what I am doing when I install new software. I know the precise configuration the space station has to be to dock with a Soyuz refill ship, but when it comes to children, we don't really know, we just give it our best shot.

It's not that you aren't a good parent, it's not that you don't rack your brain to try and figure out the best technique to use, it's just you have no idea how your children will react to what you dish out.

And this is where you can have an advantage, there is a distinct parenting benefit between those people who don't know how to parent *but* think they should. In other words, the information is out there, they just don't happen to have it. And those people who don't know how to parent *but* know it's not knowable.

Of course, there is the third group who think they know how to parent. They are not reading this book, they are crazy, sometime clinically crazy. There maybe even a fourth group, those people who really do know the secret of parenting. So far, I have never met anyone from that group, but I am hopeful.

The key to being a healthy parent in this most important profession, is to know you don't know and probably will never know. The motto of every parent is: "Where did I go wrong?"

You would think someone would figure it out? Steven Hawking the famous physicist, has a theory that time travel is not possible, as he explains, if it were possible then someone from the future would come and tell us. The fact no one has ever come from the future to tell us, must mean it's not possible. Of course you could argue that all the people who come from the future are locked away in padded cells. But that's not my point, my point is if anyone had figured out how to raise children they would have told us (I hope), and since no one has, I conclude it's just not knowable.

In parenting, you don't actually get to perfect knowledge, you just get further away from perfect ignorance.

THE UNCERTAINTY PRINCIPLE

When it comes to running a nuclear power plant certainty is a good thing, "Was it turn the blue dial to the right or the green dial to the left, oh what difference does it make, here goes...." Remember Chernobyl? When it comes to flying an F16, precision is crucial. In many, if not most things, certainty is very good. But when it comes to raising children, uncertainty makes a healthy parent.

That doesn't mean you should waver or vacillate. It doesn't mean one day this technique and another day the opposite – that's a recipe for disaster. It means that you keep to the technique that you think is your best shot all the while wondering and praying that it is working. It means being open to better ideas and looking for your mistakes.

Being clear how uncertain you are that what you are doing is effective, is the crucial element in effective parenting.

The Art of Parenting

If you need a license to fly a plane, and training to drive a car, and schooling to become a doctor, so surely you need the same to raise children?

One would think so. But parenting is not like anything else you will ever do. No amount of Dr. Spock, Dr. Phil or Dr. Who, will amount to any *real* parenting. You can't technique your way into being a good father or mother.

It's not that these parenting books don't have great ideas that can help, they often do. Let me give you a parable, being a great artist or musician requires great technique. Rembrandt, Mozart, Monet and Chopin all knew their trade well. But their greatness started after everything they learned in art or music school stopped. That gap, between where Tchaikovsky stood and everyone else stopped, is a very small gap in the world of music, but in the world of parenting, it's most of the pie.

You can't, what I call "Technique Parent."

Technique Parenting is to believe that your children are a product of the techniques you have used. Technique parents believe if they have a problem with their child, it can all be solved with the right technique. They just haven't read the right book yet.

I started to realize this was complete nonsense when my wife told me of an encounter she had with our daughter.

It went something like this. My wife was upset with our daughter and couldn't get her to see what she was doing as wrong. Finally after trying everything, my wife threw in the towel and said, "Go to your room!"

In our house that's the big punishment – I know, scary isn't it.

Anyway, my daughter didn't want to go, and asked her mother, "Why should I get punished?"

My wife answered, "Because you aren't listening!"

"Well," my daughter said, "that's not my fault."

"What do you mean, it's not your fault!?" her mother asked, incredulously.

"If you said it a different way, maybe I would understand. Why don't you try a different technique?"

My wife, in utter outrage said, "Like what!?"

"I don't know" replied my daughter, "but why don't you read that book?"

She was pointing to the book: "How to Talk so Kids will Listen" by Adele Faber and Elaine Mazlish.

My wife was blown away by my daughters creative answer and couldn't think of any way to respond....... so she let her off.

THE 80/20 RULE

The point I want to make is this, most of parenting has nothing to do with technique.

Or put a better way, technique is only 20% of what is necessary for turning out great healthy children.

The other 80% of parenting is caring.

That means, no amount of technique is going to make up for the caring a parent can give. In other words, using the best techniques will only get you so far. If you don't care, it won't really help.

And in case you were wondering, what is the proof? Easy, tell your children you don't love them. I don't think there is a parent alive who doesn't know that saying those words are in the top most destructive things you can do to a child.

Therefore you can see, that you are uniquely qualified and highly skilled to be the parent of your child, because you have what every child needs more than any technique. Despite all your inadequacies (we all have them), your shortfalls, you stress and emotional insecurities, with all this we nevertheless can see the Divine plan. Children are born to the parents who are uniquely qualified to raise their children – because parents care and no one will care more than them.

So, if you want to do a do a better job as a parent, care more.

CARING AND LOVING

Don't confuse the two. Everyone loves their children, even the workaholic who never sees them.

But that isn't what your children want or need (true, it's better than nothing.)

What they need is caring.

Caring is time, caring is effort.

I recently went to visit my son who just went away to school. He was feeling a little homesick and so my wife told me "I think it would be a good idea to visit." My schedule was packed but my wife has good intuition on these things so I flew up to see him. The trip took me a whole day, yet because of the distances and time in the air, I was only able to spend an hour with him.

Would he have liked me to spend more time? Probably yes. Did he <u>need</u> me to spend more time? I don't think so. My trip told him I cared. Children need to know someone cares about them.

Caring is the magic ingredient. You can have the worst techniques, but if you really care, it won't be that bad. Alternatively, you could seemingly have the best parents, the best environment, and the best techniques, and you will still have problematic children, if you don't care.

In other words, if your child is going through a particular problem, we are led to believe that all you have to do is look it up in an encyclopedia of kids problems, apply it, like some kind of medicine, and you should have instant results!

I hope you understand, that is not going to happen. In fact, if your child is going through a particularly difficult time and letting you know it, one of the first questions you have to ask yourself is, did I care enough?

EFFECTIVE CARING

Just because you do care, doesn't always mean your child sees it as such. I know parents who care more than anything I can imagine. But for whatever reason, the children mis-understood the caring for something else. They didn't see it as caring. Sometimes a tragedy occurs, or a change in priorities and the caring seems to the child as less.

"The First Child Syndrome" is this. When a family has a second child, the first child perceives the lesser love, not as lesser love, but as not caring, even hate.

Caring is no simple matter. It's not a Hallmark card or a big birthday party. Sometimes caring can mean doing things that make your children scream the roof off. I remember very clearly, as a little boy my father taking me in the middle of the night to the hospital for a procedure that scared the living daylights out of me (I was not very fond of doctors as a child – nothing personal) – boy, did I scream; the whole hospital heard me. But I knew my father cared, and he knew I knew.

You have to be able to see what you are giving from the vantage point of your child. How will they think of it. This is no easy thing, and your spouse will often be able to give you another perspective. However, the more you try to understand, in of itself, is a sign of caring and will bear positive fruits.

One of the saddest stories that I ever experienced, was when a student of mine, let's call him Jonathan, told me of something he had said to his mother over 50 years ago when he was a child.

Jonathan's story went like this. 50 years prior, Jonathan was playing in the sand box at his friends house, Simon. Simon's mother came out and told Simon to come inside, "Dinner is ready," she said.

Simon turned to Jonathan and said, quite matter-of-factly, "Keep playing, 3."

Jonathan didn't know what Simon meant by "3," but he kept on playing.

Soon, Simon's mother was out again. This time she was clearly agitated and shouted to Simon to come in or there would be consequences.

Simon again turned to Jonathan and simply said, "That's 2, keep playing."

So, they did.

After a few minutes, Simon's mother was at it again and this time she was screaming, "Simon, if you don't get in here right now, it's bed without dinner, and a good spanking to boot!"

Simon turned to Jonathan and said, "That's 3, got to go."

And off Simon went. He understood that Simon's mother said everything in 3's and as long as you didn't go over the 3, you were fine.

Anyway, Jonathan went home, walked into the kitchen to find his mother preparing dinner. Then he said something that for 50 years he would always remember, yet he never understood what he himself meant, "Mom, why don't you shout at me?"

Jonathan, understood the contradiction, why would anyone ask to be shouted at? What did he really mean?

Freud explained it. Freud said, "The opposite of love is not hate, it's indifference." Indifference says "I don't care, I don't love you."

Jonathan came to understand that he was really asking his mother, "Why don't you care about me?"

If she cared she would get angry now and again. We only get angry when we care.

In Jonathan's case, the lack of shouting was showing Jonathan a lack of love.

DEEPER

Should you shout at your children, get angry and scream?

No.

But listen to what Jonathan is saying. Even though on the surface of it no child wants to hear his mother shout at him, nevertheless even with that bad technique, if the child understands that it's coming from a place of caring, then the child will be better off for it.

In a similar way, you take your child for an immunization shot. Does the child like it? Of course not. But in the long run, it's good for them and they will appreciate it.

In other words, "losing it" with your children is good for them. That does not mean you should feel good about it, and it doesn't mean you should not try as hard as you can to minimize the times you lose it. But losing it, is a clear sign in the sky, "I care about you."

23 packs of wolves could take up residence in your home while you are out of town and you would come back and merely shrug it off to bad luck and proceed to do what is necessary to clean it up. But your son spills the grape juice on your new carpet

and you blow your top. When it comes to people we care about we are more apt to lose control.

Many people who have lost a parent look back now in fondness to the times their parent scolded them.

I would even put it another way. Our children's need to feel cared for is so deep and profound, that they will almost inevitably push you to the point you will lost it. In other words, unless you really don't care, it is almost impossible that your children will not push you over the proverbial ledge.

I think it's true to say, that every parent expresses at some time, and sometimes often, the concept, "you are driving me crazy." After all we have now learned together, I think we can see, that "you are driving me crazy," is a clear sign both parent and child are doing their jobs!

So, in conclusion, technique is not a waste of time, and in fact you should always be striving to improve your technique. After all, 20% of $100million is still a lot of money. 20% added on to a good parent will give you remarkable children. However, the real pay-off is in the amount of effort you put into caring.

Chapter 9:
Marriage is NOT Parenting

Whenever you get off the Highway, as you approach the exit, you will notice there are a lot of signs warning you to lower your speed.

"Why do they do that?"

Simple, it takes time to get used to the change of pace. After dealing with children, people need some warning to realize the change of pace before they start relating to their spouse.

The same is true if you are coming from the office, it's a change to now deal with your spouse. Don't talk to your spouse the way you talk to your assistant or your children.

That change is very crucial, because as we have explained 80% of an effective relationship with a child is caring and 20% is technique. But, and this is a huge BUT, with a marriage it's the mirror image.

Effective marriage is 80% technique and 20% caring.

With marriage as opposed to parenting, caring will only get you so far, the most important thing to focus on is technique. In other words, the emphasis most put on technique when it comes to parenting will not reap the great rewards you are looking for in your children, but if you apply that same effort to your marriage, you would be so happily married most people who met you would think you were on medication.

In marriage, it doesn't matter how much you care, if you forget your wife's birthday you are toast. If you leave your husbands car in a mess, you will have big problems. Do you care about your wife? I hope so. Does how you treat his car reflect how you care about him? I hope not. The reason you are going to be in trouble is you are ignorant of the technique of what your spouse needs.

With marriage it's all down to when you say it, how you say it and how often you say it. It takes a lifetime to figure out how to tell your wife which dress looks better and how to answer the question, "do I look fat to you?" when she's eight months pregnant. My wife uses the skill of a brain surgeon, when she tells me it's time to get your act together. She's got the technique down (and don't I know it), with just the right amount of praise and correction. When she wants me to do something, I don't even see it coming.

Similarly, I have no idea why, when I bring my wife flowers, I did a good thing. If someone bought me flowers, I would think they were weird. But, it works with my wife – it's a technique I have learned – one of many.

With children, the caring is the most important thing and it gets through <u>despite</u> the bad technique. With a spouse, if you have a bad technique nothing will get through, NOTHING!

If your husband or wife doesn't hear what you are saying, you have to figure out a way to get them to listen. Or, you must figure out a way to say it that they can hear. That is technique. Otherwise, nothing will change.

Singing your children's praises to them, is a good technique, and as such will not get you very far in getting them to do their homework on a consistent basis. But, doing similar every time your husband takes out the garbage will do wonders for your love life.

Now, isn't it interesting, that when it comes to our children, we will read book after book on improving our technique. But, with a spouse we will be lucky if we read the Peanuts comic strip.

Not only that, but there aren't many books to read. A mother recently told me she read the book "How to Talk so Kids will Listen," and used the ideas on her husband (successfully!)

There is no book, "How to talk so husbands will listen."

But the truth is, it isn't that difficult. Because with children it's a mystery how to communicate. Even when they seem to listen, you have no idea if it got through.

I can't tell you how many times I or my wife have had a heart-to-heart with one of the kids, where they nod at the right places and agree to change. Then in the debriefing with the other spouse, we will both admit, we have no idea whether the child in question really got it. With a spouse, all you have to do is ask. A spouse will tell you clearly, "I don't understand what you are talking about."

If your spouse has a high school education or less they are more than well equipped to tell you <u>exactly</u> how they would like everything.

Not only that, <u>you</u> can tell your spouse EXACTLY what you want them to do as well.

"Wow, is it that easy?"

Unfortunately, no.

You see, next time your spouse gets angry at you, ask them what you should have done differently. Then the next time, if you don't do it in the precise way that they explained it, shame on you. But if you did, one of two things will happen:

1) It will work and you will live happily ever after.

"Really?"

No, this isn't very likely, but miracles happen.

2) Your spouse will still get angry with you.

But that's OK, it just means *they* didn't really know what *they* wanted – very typical of us all. So, point out that you did exactly as was requested and you still got yelled at – this might engender some sympathy (not very likely), gratitude (ditto), denial or "well you should know what I really want!"

Either way, ask again, "Next time how should I do it?" Maybe even write down the answer.

Just keep going and eventually you will both, together, figure out the technique that works. It's a journey of self discovery.

That discovery will bear great fruits. You will find out how to communicate with each other. It may take a few dry runs, you might get a little frustrated, but the end is glorious. Don't give up, it is so worth it.

KEY ISSUES

A lot of spouses when they try and resolve a dispute get caught in what I call, "TUNS."

TUNS stands for "The United Nations Syndrome."

What they try to do is prove that they were right, and of course, their partner was wrong.

Just like The United Nations.

This is an exercise in futility. For your marriage, and probably for The United Nations too.

Why?

Because in the history of the world, nobody has ever proved to their spouse that they were wrong (same is true in The United Nations).

Ok, I exaggerate a little (only when it comes to a spouse), but the point is, the issues between spouses rarely have anything to do with right or wrong, even when morality is at the core of the dispute.

Marital disputes almost always revolve around trying to understand what makes your spouse tick – and what makes you tick.

Instead of asking the question, "how do I show my husband he is wrong?" Ask, "What do I have to do to get him to change?"

Don't try and get him/her to admit they were wrong; get them to change.

Let me clarify. I was recently asked to resolve a dispute between a husband and wife. They had an issue that seemed to them (and me) was going nowhere.

The wife, Joanne, was very upset with her husband because he refused to drive in a way that she considered safe. He of course, being of the male persuasion, was forbidden by genetic encoding to take criticism from anyone about his driving, especially his wife.

It went back and forth, about the "correct" way to drive, and what the law says, and I am sure it would have eventually landed in the Supreme Court.

After I had heard the arguments repeated for the 900th time, I stopped them and turned to Joanne, and said, "Listen, you really want your husband to drive differently, right?"

"Of course!" she said.

"OK, well instead of trying to paint him into a corner and prove to him he is an unsafe driver, which is akin to killing a husband," (joke), "why don't you ask him, what would it take, or what would you have to do, to get him to drive the way you would like?"

So, right there she asked him that very question.

It's a very funny thing, his whole mood changed and he gave her a list of two or three things.

She thought about it, they negotiated a little, and he said, "I can do that."

And the argument was over.

Now, not all arguments can be resolved that way. Not everything has a price. But the point is, ask your question in a way that your spouse can help you find the answer. Trying to find a way for you both to live together in peace is so much better, for you and The United Nations.

It's a Journey

The really meaningful things in life are journeys, not destinations. Anything meaningful can always be improved.

Raising children is meaningful because you never get to an end point. The same is true with marriage. As long as you have a healthy marriage, there will always be things you can do better.

Chapter 9:
Forgive and Forget

I am sure that just about every newlywed has received this piece of advice, be careful of what you say, because you can forgive, but never forget.

If that were true I think we would all put our children up for adoption. If we didn't forgive *and* forget what they do to us, we would need ledgers bigger than Enrons' schemes to keep track of all the grievances.

With our children we not only forget the worst, horrendous abuses they inflict upon us, and barely ask for an apology. But, if we do remember, we look back on those abuses with fondness.

How often will parents look through a photo album and recount, with a little tear in their eye, "The vacation from Hell!" "Oh yes, look there Judy, that's where our little Jimmy drove the station wagon off the side of the cliff....doesn't he look cute behind the wheel? I still can't bend my left index finger because I broke it pulling him out at the last moment.....oh, those were the good old days."

Yet that same person, if his wife gets a scratch on the car, he will give her a list going back to the stone age of all the times she, her mother and her ancestors mistreated the family chariot. He will claim so-called scientific evidence that she is genetically engineered to not be safe behind a wheel!

With our spouses, we *might* forgive, but rarely do we forget. With our children we can, and do, forgive *and* forget, **ALL THE TIME.**

NOT ONLY THAT

I remember a story of a student of mine. We will call her Jessica. She told me of an incident that happened while she was playing with her 6 year old daughter in the pool. Her daughter turned to her and said, "Mommy, I don't like you anymore!"

Children say the darnedest things.

So, I asked Jessica, "What did you do?'

"Well," Jessica answered, "I took her aside and explained to her that you just don't say those kind of things to your mother."

And, everything worked out.

So then I asked Jessica, what would have happened if your husband came home one day and as you opened the door to greet him, he turned to you and said, "Honey, I've been thinking, I don't love you anymore!'

Well, you could have peeled Jessica off the ceiling. She was very clear about her reaction to something like that, and it wasn't pleasant.

Without going into the details, let your imagination go wild and consider the different ways you could employ a sledgehammer. You get the idea.

So, then I asked Jessica. Okay, lets say right after that, he turns to you and says, "You know honey, I have no idea why I said that. I have had the most horrendous day. My car overheated on the Freeway. My boss was on my case all day long, three clients cancelled their orders and my stocks are in the toilet. It's just been one of those days. Lets just forget I ever said it?"

Jessica laughed, actually she only broke a small hint of a smile, as if to say, "forget it – you are in the dog house, buddy!"

When it comes to children, we forgive and forget -- easily.

EASILY

How many times have one of your children done something wrong to you, and you told them to say sorry?

"But I'm not sorry?" the child says.

"Never mind, just say the words," you reply.

"No!" the child says again.

"Whisper it in my ear," you plead with them.

"No!'

"Write it in the air, anything!"

With children *we want* to forgive them. With spouses we want an apology in blood, tattooed on their arm -- engraved in stone around their neck.

We want them to pay, big time.

You **CAN** forgive and forget -- you do it all the time…. with your children.

It's not your spouses' fault that you can't forgive them easily. It's not the words they need to find or the remorse they have to express.

It's your inability to get over it --- it's your problem.

Ponder this idea next time you get upset with your spouse. You will notice how much longer you fume and pout, emotions you never experience with your children when they upset you.

Why is that?

Because it has nothing to do with your spouse. True they did something they shouldn't, but so did your children. The extra emotion is your problem. And if it's your problem, don't make your spouse suffer for it.

WE SUFFER MORE

The reason we want to forgive our children is that we understand that by not forgiving them, we suffer.

We suffer, not our children. Try not talking to your children because they did something wrong. I don't know if they would even notice. But for sure, they will not suffer as much as you will.

This is true with your spouse too. By holding on to all the things your spouse has done to you, it is not as damaging to your spouse as it is to you.

Holding on to grievances, is stopping you from having the most wonderful blissful relationship you could possibly imagine.

Living happily ever after is very attainable, if you will only learn to forgive and forget.

Just remember, it's up to you.

Chapter 10:
Conclusion: The Bliss Mission

Divorce and unhappy marriages are the single largest causes of poverty in America. Children grow up in abusive households or homes with a single parent. In this environment, children find school difficult and often academic achievement is minimized.

50% divorce rates are not just a personal tragedy, they are a drain on the financial well-being of the country. Increased welfare, foster care, loss of work, depression, etc., take away from the normal operations of a country.

But the greatest impact is that the cycle continues, the children themselves continue in the patterns of their parents.

The wisdom of running a moderately happy home, and even one in Bliss, is not as difficult as it is lacking.

Now after 15 years, what began as a small group of students, has grown into the "Bliss" movement attracting national and international attention.

By reading, applying and sharing these ideas, our mission is to reduce the divorce rate to single digits.

We invite you to join our mission.

_____ THE END OF THE BEGINNING _____

518561

Made in the USA